BUSES AND COACHES
IN WALES
1980 TO 2001

MIKE STREET

AMBERLEY

First published 2020

Amberley Publishing
The Hill, Stroud
Gloucestershire, GL5 4EP

www.amberley-books.com

Copyright © Mike Street, 2020

The right of Mike Street to be identified as
the Author of this work has been asserted in
accordance with the Copyrights, Designs and
Patents Act 1988.

ISBN 978 1 3981 0159 3 (print)
ISBN 978 1 3981 0160 9 (ebook)

British Library Cataloguing in Publication Data.
A catalogue record for this book is available from
the British Library.

Origination by Amberley Publishing.
Printed in the UK.

Introduction

The Author

I have lived in Cardiff since my birth in 1953. My interest in buses started in 1965 when a classmate at high school produced a copy of Ian Allan's *British Bus Fleets* book. Photography followed in 1968, firstly in black and white, followed by colour slide, then colour print and finally digital from 2002. After a thirty-three-year career in local government (finance and IT, not transport!), early retirement in 2004 gave me the opportunity to commence scanning the 20,000 plus photographs I have taken over the years.

When I started photographing buses I tended to concentrate on the major operators and new vehicles of the smaller operators. One Sunday when photographing in the coach park at Porthcawl I was accosted by a driver who wanted to know why I didn't photograph his coach. I said that I was not interested in the older vehicles, just the newer ones. His reply was that the newer ones would be there next year, but the older ones could have been sold on or even gone for scrap and then I would have missed them. I took his words to heart and just wish I'd also started to photograph the minibuses that were around at the time!

When asked by Amberley's Connor Stait if I'd like to produce a second volume, thinking that I wouldn't have enough photographs for a shorter time frame, I said I'd cover all of Wales from 1980 to 2001. However, on looking through my collection, I found almost 1,000 relevant photographs – so it has been a hard job to select the required number of images which, I hope, will be of interest to the reader.

The Area

My first book covered South East Wales (i.e. the counties of Gwent, Mid, South and West Glamorgan) in the 1970s. As mentioned above, this volume includes vehicles operated between 1980 and 2001 from fleets in the eight counties that constituted Wales between 1974 and 1996. Thus, in addition to the four South East Wales counties, Clwyd in the north east, Gwynedd in the north west, Dyfed in the west and Powys in central Wales are included. These eight counties were abolished and replaced by twenty-two county or county borough unitary authorities from April 1996. This volume ignores that Local Government Reorganisation and refers to the eight 1974 to 1996 counties throughout.

Again, the selection of photographs is very much a personal one, though I have tried to include a broad cross-section of operators and vehicle types, the emphasis being on the smaller, independent operators rather than the municipal and National Bus Company operators. I admit that there are large gaps in my photographic collection, as visits outside South East Wales were quite rare in this period, due to health issues and work commitments.

The Major Operators

The following is a brief outline of the main changes to the major (i.e. council and former National Bus Company) operators in Wales during the period under review.

The 1974 Local Government Reorganisation had seen Aberdare UDC becoming part of Cynon Valley Borough Council; the UDCs of Bedwas & Machen, Caerphilly and Gelligaer merging as part of Rhymney Valley District Council; Pontypridd UDC becoming part of Taff-Ely Borough Council; the West Mon Omnibus Board becoming part of Islwyn Borough Council and, in North Wales, the UDCs of Colwyn Bay and Llandudno merging to form Aberconwy Borough Council. Control of the larger County Borough Council fleets of Cardiff, Merthyr Tydfil and Newport remained unchanged.

Deregulation of bus services in October 1986 required local authorities to relinquish control of their bus fleets; this was initially achieved by creating 'arms-length' companies which were still under the control of the local authorities. Subsequent developments were as follows: Conwy CBC (successor to Aberconwy BC from April 1996) closed in March 2000; Cynon Valley Transport sold to Western Travel subsidiary Red & White in August 1992; Inter Valley Link (successor to Rhymney Valley DC from October 1986) sold to National Welsh in April 1989; Merthyr Tydfil Transport ceased in October 1989; Taff-Ely Transport sold to National Welsh in November 1988. City of Cardiff Transport Ltd (Cardiff Bus), Islwyn Borough Transport Ltd (owned by Caerphilly CBC from April 1996) and Newport Transport Ltd survived into the new millennium. The only change since has seen the sale of Islwyn Borough Transport Ltd to Red & White in January 2010.

Crosville Motor Services Ltd was split in September 1986, the North Wales area becoming Crosville Wales Ltd with headquarters at Llandudno Junction; it was sold to Arriva in 1998 and was renamed Arriva Cymru. South Wales Transport became part of the Badgerline group following deregulation and acquired a number of small operators. It set up a separate coaching unit, United Welsh Coaches, which operated between December 1988 and September 1992 when it was merged with the Brewer fleet. The merger of the Badgerline group and the Grampian Regional Transport group to form Firstbus led to South Wales Transport becoming First Cymru in 1999; The National Welsh Omnibus Co., which had been formed in 1978, was subject to a management buy-out, but was placed in administration and closed down in April 1992. Prior to this, in January 1991, Red & White Services Ltd was formed to take over operation of the Gwent area of National Welsh, including depots at Brynmawr, Brecon, Cwmbran, Chepstow, Crosskeys and Ross-on-Wye. This company soon became part of the Western Travel group and by 1994 had become part of the Stagecoach group, operating as Stagecoach in South Wales on the Red & White licence. In February 1992, Tellings-Golden Miller's Cardiff operation acquired Bedwas and Porth depots and formed Rhondda Buses Ltd to continue operations. Rhondda Buses Ltd was then acquired by Stagecoach in December 1997 and merged with the Red & White subsidiary from January 1998. On the closure of National Welsh, operations in the Bridgend area were taken over by South Wales Transport and those in the Barry and Penarth areas of the Vale of Glamorgan by Cardiff Bus.

This publication covers the former National Bus Company fleets and their successors up to the time vehicles started to be painted in their new (i.e. Arriva, First and Stagecoach) group liveries.

The Independent Operators

There was much change to the independent operators in the last quarter of the twentieth century. Some operators of stage carriage services were subject to relentless competition by larger operators and subsequently sold out to them, while new operators came in to run services deemed not profitable enough by the larger operators or run with a subsidy from the relevant local authority. Jones (Shamrock) of Pontypridd acquired a number of other operators in the 1990s, the best-known being Thomas Motors of Barry. Jones and Bebb Travel of Llantwit Fardre (along with operators in the Swansea area) would later become part of the ill-fated Veolia empire. The fate of some of the smaller operators is mentioned in the captions to the photographs.

The Vehicles

The New Bus Grant introduced by the government in the 1970s enabled operators to buy new vehicles at a discount for use on stage carriage services – this grant was not confined to buses, but coaches with driver-operated doors and fittings for ticket machines also qualified as long as they spent 50 per cent of their mileage on stage carriage services. Thus, many older vehicles were replaced by new ones in the 1970s and 1980s. At the start of the period most vehicles were still of British manufacture, but Volvo and Scania had started to gain a foothold in the coach market and bodywork from the likes of Berkhof, Caetano, Jonckheere, and Van Hool were becoming more common. Dennis had re-entered the PSV market in the late 1970s and its Dart and later Dart SLF single-deckers were a popular choice, with over 12,000 being built between

1998 and 2008 when it was superseded by the equally popular Enviro series. Bedford and Ford, who were well known for their lightweight chassis, both ceased production in the 1980s, but Ford continued to build its Transit minibus which became popular with many fleets following deregulation of bus services in 1986. Bodybuilder Duple closed down in the 1980s, with Plaxton taking on production of the 320 coach and Marshall the Dartline body on the Dennis Dart chassis.

The Locations

Many of the photographs were taken in the Cardiff area, but a holiday to Llandudno in September 2000 gave an opportunity to photograph some of the North Wales vehicles. Other holidays to Scotland, the south coast of England and Lincolnshire (for the Spalding Flower Festival) often produced coaches from Wales. Events nearer to home, producing a significant number of coaches, included the Michael Jackson concert held at Cardiff's National Stadium in July 1988, Garden Festival Wales at Ebbw Vale in the summer of 1992, and the 'Cor y Byd' (Choir of the World) events at the National Stadium in May 1992 and May 1993. Photographs from some of these events are included here.

Acknowledgements

My thanks to my family and friends for their understanding when I would suddenly 'disappear from view' to take a photograph of a bus which had suddenly appeared! Thanks also to the various operators who, in the days of Health & Safety legislation, were still willing to allow access to premises to take photographs.

Once again, thanks to my wife, Carole, and mother-in-law, Betty, for allowing me the time to produce this book.

Acknowledgement is due to BusView and Bus Lists on the Web, whose information has proved invaluable in researching the details and histories of the vehicles, to various online sites which have filled in many gaps in my knowledge. Finally, thanks to Connor Stait at Amberley Publishing for the impetus to write this book and to the staff at Amberley for organising it into a publishable format.

Mike Street
Cardiff
February 2020

Municipal (Council) and Former Municipal Fleets

New as Cardiff 502 in January 1983, RBO 502Y was a Leyland Olympian ONLXB/1R with an East Lancs H43/31F body. When photographed in July 1988 it was carrying this all-over advert for Newport's B&Q Autocentre. Sold to McConn, Rathcoole, in the Irish Republic in April 1998, it was re-registered 83-D-4130 and then converted to open-top in 2002.

Cardiff operated a small fleet of coaches, mostly for private hire work; however, number 5 (B905 DHB), a 1985 Leyland Tiger TRCTL11/3R with Duple Caribbean 2 C53FT body, was seen in June 1994 about to depart for Aberystwyth on the short-lived 'Cambrian Express'. Cardiff's coaching operations were sold to Brewer in October 1995 and B905 DHB became Brewer's number 179.

The last vehicles delivered to Cardiff before the October 1986 privatisation were PMT B20F-bodied Mercedes Benz L608Ds 111–2 (D111–2 LTG). 112 was caught in January 1987 carrying its original livery with Cardiff Minibus fleet name and Pick an Orange strap line. It passed to an Irish operator in September 1994 and was re-registered 86-LH-1096.

Cardiff Bus took delivery of fifteen Optare Excel L1150s in 1997, 201–15 (R201–15 DKG). They were low-floor buses and carried EasyRider lettering. Not popular in Cardiff, all fifteen were sold to Reading in 2000 with 206–15 then passing to Eastbourne in late 2001/early 2002 and 201–5 being exported to New Zealand in 2005.

New to Cynon Valley BC in December 1975 as fleet number 16, Leyland-National 10351/1R LDW 361P had passed to Cynon Valley Transport by the time this photograph was taken in July 1988. The change of livery, from all-over maroon, was due to the appointment of a new manager in 1986. LDW 361P passed to Red & White as number 435 in August 1992.

New to Cynon Valley BC in May 1986, number 5 (C604 KVP) was a Freight Rover Sherpa 350 with Carlyle B16F bodywork and was seen in Cardiff that July. Renumbered 39 in February 1988, it had a short life with Cynon Valley, passing to Arrowline, Knutsford by July 1988.

E291 TAX, a Renault S56 with Northern Counties DP25F bodywork, was new to
Cynon Valley Transport as fleet number 1 in March 1988. Photographed in Merthyr
Tydfil bus station on 16 August 1992, the 'Now we're Red & White' poster in the
windscreen is a result of CVT selling out to Red & White on 5 August, operations
being continued by a new subsidiary, The Valleys Bus Co. Ltd.

Inter Valley Link 30 (C30 EUH), a Leyland Olympian ONTL11/2R with East Lancs
CH47/31F bodywork, had been new to Rhymney Valley DC in September 1985,
passing to IVL in October 1986. Photographed in Cardiff bus station on 19 November
1988, the bus passed to Stevensons of Uttoxeter in April 1989.

Inter Valley Link 98 (FYX 822W), a Leyland Leopard PSU3E/4R with Duple Dominant II Express C49F coachwork, had been new to Grey Green of London N16 in 1981, passing to IVL in March 1988. Photographed in Caerphilly bus station in June 1988, it passed to National Welsh as number UD1198 in April 1989.

In October 1988, Inter Valley Link placed seventeen coach-seated Optare Metroriders into service, 101–17 (F101–17 YWO), in a new livery and with 'Inter Valley Classic' branding. Three, headed by 105 (F105 YWO), were waiting to enter National Welsh's Bedwas House Industrial Estate depot on Sunday 23 April 1989 following the take-over by that company.

The first vehicles delivered new to Islwyn Borough Transport Ltd were East Lancs DP47F-bodied Leyland Tiger TRBTL11/2Rs 44–6 (D44–6 MBO) which entered service in October 1986. 46 (D46 MBO) was seen in Cardiff bus station in May 1987 operating the service to Tredegar which, in earlier days, had been jointly operated by Caerphilly UDC, Cardiff Corporation and the West Mon Omnibus Board. Islwyn Borough Transport was the direct descendent of the latter.

Islwyn Borough Transport purchased its first coach in 1988 and acquired the Walters Coaches (Paul Diaper Eurotours), Newport, business with two coaches in 1991. One of these coaches was this Mercedes-Benz 0303/15R C49FT which had been new in 1985 to Paul Diaper registered C722 RJU. It passed to Walters in 1986 and was re-registered DIA 4800 in 1988; Islwyn re-registered it SIB 6740 in 1995 and sold it in 2000. It was on tour in Falmouth when photographed in September 1997.

New in December 1995, Islwyn Borough Transport's 12 (N573 OUH) was a Mercedes Benz Vario 811D with Plaxton Beaver B29F bodywork. Seen in Cardiff bus station in September 1996 it was operating the Cardiff to Tredegar service. Following the Local Government Reorganisation of April 1996, Islwyn Borough Transport Ltd passed to the control of Caerphilly Borough Council.

Llandudno UDC bought Waveney B20F-bodied Guy Wolf JC 5313 in 1938 and sold it for preservation in 1965. I never visited Llandudno while the council-operated buses were running, but the fleet was too interesting to ignore! JC 5313 (and Roberts-bodied Wolf JC 2772) were at a preserved vehicle rally at Cardiff City Hall in June 1984.

The Great Orme Tramway in Llandudno is Britain's only cable-hauled public road tramway, it opened on 31 July 1902 and is to 3-ft 6-in. gauge. The bottom section is operated by cars four and five, the original 1902 Hurst Nelson 37-ft bogie cars; the top section by similar cars six and seven. Here, car four is seen leaving the upper station of the bottom section in September 2000. At this time the top section was closed for renovation in preparation for the centenary in 2002.

Merthyr Tydfil bought six Leyland National NL106L11/1R B41F buses in 1980, numbered 221–6 (GHB 221–6W), they passed to Merthyr Tydfil Transport Ltd in October 1986 and 223 was caught in Merthyr bus station in May 1987. All six passed to National Welsh in September 1989 but were not operated, 223 moving to a Merseyside operator by January 1990.

In 1985 Merthyr Tydfil exchanged three 1979 Marshall-bodied Dennis Dominators for three of Chester's 1976 Duple Dominant bus-bodied Leyland Leopard PSU4D/2Rs. 241 (TMB 878R) had been number 78 in the Chester fleet and was photographed in Merthyr bus station in March 1989; this bus passed to Parfitts, Rhymney Bridge in September 1989.

Merthyr Tydfil Transport Ltd's 103/6 (D103/6 NDW) were Leyland B51F-bodied Lynx LX112TL11ZR1Rs new in April 1987 and were photographed in the town's bus station the following month. In late 1989 both found new owners in the London area.

Merthyr Tydfil Transport Ltd bought five B23F-bodied MCW Metroriders in early 1989. 105 was part of a cancelled order for SUT, Sheffield, and carried registration F105 CWG on delivery to Merthyr, being re-registered F505 CBO before entering service in February. It passed to City of Oxford Motor Services in October 1989.

New to Newport in May 1980, MCW H46/31F-bodied Metrobus 70 (DTG 370V) was seen in the town's high street in June 1987. DTG 370V was sold to Cowie, Stamford Hill, in 1992, later operating in open-top form at Stratford-upon-Avon. The bus's destination, Spytty Park, would in the future be developed as an out-of-town retail park.

In 1983 Newport bought 10–18 (RUH 10–18Y), Scania BR112DH double-decker chassis fitted with Wadham Stringer forty-two-seat single-decker bodywork. Number 10 (RUH 10Y) was seen at Barry Island in June 1996, it was sold to Black Prince of Morley in West Yorkshire (along with 14–6/8) in 1998.

In 1998 Newport Borough Transport Ltd replaced the Wadham Stringer-bodied Scanias, numbered 10–18, with Wright B46F-bodied Scania L94UBs registered S110, 211, 112–8 TDW. Here, number 11 (S211 TDW) is seen in Cardiff bus station in April 2006. Unfortunately, my visits to Newport were few and far between at this time.

New to Taff-Ely BC in March 1984, Dennis Lancet SD515 36 (A36 XBO) had an East Lancs B47F body. It passed to National Welsh in November 1988 and was later with Rhondda Buses. It was seen in Taff Street, Pontypridd, when new. Note the price of Kelloggs Cornflakes (59.5p) in Tesco!

Taff-Ely Transport Ltd bought dealer-registered Wadham Stringer-bodied Leyland Swift 60 (E961 PME) in June 1988, it was seen at the depot when new. Sold in October of the same year, it later operated on Jersey, in Merthyr Tydfil and on Guernsey where I caught up with it again in June 2001.

National Bus Company (and former NBC) Fleets

New to Crosville as number CLL318 in July 1976, RMA 318P was a Leyland Leopard PSU3C/4R with a Plaxton Supreme III Express C49F body. It had been fitted for one-man operation and renumbered ELL318 by the time I photographed it in Dolgellau in June 1980 on Traws Cambria route 700 to Bangor. The coach passed to Crosville Wales in September 1986 and was sold in March 1991.

Crosville SLL635 (OCA 635P) was a Bristol LH6L with ECW B43F body new in March 1976. It was seen in Caernarfon in July 1982, en route to Dinorwic, carrying a Snowdon Sherpa slip board. It was sold in May 1984, before the formation of Crosville Wales, and ended its days in Malta.

Crosville ELL335 (JMB 335T) was parked up at Barmouth in July 1982. It was a Duple Dominant Express C49F-bodied Leyland Leopard PSU3E/4R new in March 1979 numbered CLL335. It passed to Crosville Wales in September 1986 and was sold in July 1988.

Crosville DVG551 (WHN 415G) was a 1969 Bristol VRT/SL6G with ECW H39/31F bodywork acquired from United Automobile, where it had been numbered 605, in February 1982. It was seen in Aberystwyth in July 1982 carrying DeCambria branding; it was withdrawn in March 1985.

Transferred to Crosville Wales in September 1986, forty-four-seat Leyland National 10351B/1R SNL563 (HMA 563T) had been new to Crosville in December 1978. It was seen in Chester bus station in September 1992 and was withdrawn in June 1997.

Also seen in Chester bus station in September 1992, Crosville Wales DVL412 (ODM 412V) was a Bristol VRT/SL3/501 with ECW H43/31F bodywork new to Crosville in September 1979. It was ready to depart on the 24-mile journey to Llangollen.

Reeve Burgess Beaver-bodied Mercedes Benz 709D MMM351 (G151 FJC) was new to Crosville Wales in September 1989 and lasted in the fleet until August 2000. Again, it was seen in Chester in September 1992. The Y Ddraig Fach lettering is Welsh for The Little Dragon.

Crosville Wales acquired CVV328 (D328 VVV), a 1987 Jonckheere Jubilee P599 C51FT-bodied Volvo B10M-61, from Tellings-Golden Miller's Cardiff operation in August 1993. Used on the long Traws Cambria coach network, it was seen in Cardiff bus station soon after acquisition.

National Welsh MUH 285X was a Leyland Olympian ONLXB/1R with ECW H45/32F bodywork; new in March 1982 with fleet number HR1855, it was renumbered HR855 in February 1986. Photographed in Cardiff bus station in August 1990, it had just been repainted in the new, post-privatisation, National Welsh livery. The bus passed to Rhondda Buses in August 1992.

National Welsh 2 (C102 HKG) was one of the first batch of minibuses purchased; it was a Robin Hood sixteen-seat Ford Transit new in February 1986 and was photographed in Windsor Road, Penarth, three years later. In May 1992 it passed to Rhondda Buses.

Surprising additions to the National Welsh fleet in 1987 were DAF MB200s XC265–8 (D625–8 YCX) with Plaxton Paramount 3500 Mk III C51FT coachwork. D628 YCX was seen carrying Ski STS (School Travel Service) livery in Cardiff bus station in August 1989, after being renumbered XC968. It was re-registered AKG 293A by May 1991 and passed to Tellings-Golden Miller in July 1992.

Following the acquisition of Taff-Ely Transport Ltd in September 1988, six Freight Rover Sherpa 405D minibuses entered service with National Welsh in Pontypridd in a Taff-Ely Bustler livery carrying Carlyle twenty-seat bodywork. 226 (F226 AWO) was seen in Taff Street, Pontypridd, in July 1989. The Taff Vale Centre behind the bus is currently being redeveloped.

New to Taff-Ely BC as number 24 in May 1977, Leyland National 11351A/1R RBO 24R passed to National Welsh as fleet number N655 in November 1988. When seen in Caerphilly bus station in March 1989, it had been transferred to Bedwas depot and carried Caerphilly Buslink livery. It was sold to local operator Glyn Williams of Cross Keys in January 1991.

The last vehicles delivered to National Welsh were five Volvo B10M-60s with Plaxton Paramount 3500 Expressliner coachwork – XC969–73 (G969–73 KTX). XC969/70 were parked at Cwmbran depot in early July 1990, before entering service. Both passed to Tellings-Golden Miller in February 1992 then to Express Travel, Perth, in May 1992.

Red & White LR714 (GTX 738W) had been transferred from National Welsh in February 1991; it was a 1980 Bristol VRT/SL3/501 with ECW H43/31F bodywork. It was seen in Cardiff bus station in July 1991 laying over after the 40-mile journey from Abergavenny. It remained in the fleet until September 1998.

Red & White 914 (AAX 516A) was a Leyland Tiger TRCTL11/3R with a Plaxton Paramount 3200 C48FT body, which had been new to National Welsh in July 1983 with registration SDW 930Y and fleet number UC1214. It received its new registration from Bristol Lodekka driver-trainer T1063 (which had originally carried registration 20 AAX) in July 1987 and passed to Red & White in February 1991.

New to Red & White as number 312 in September 1992, K312 YKG was a Mercedes Benz 811D with Wright B33F bodywork. Seen in Cardiff in February 1993, it stayed in the fleet until September 2002.

Red & White 360 (GBO 246W) was a Leyland Leopard PSU4E/2R with a Duple Dominant Bus B47F body, which had been new to Hill's, Tredegar, in 1981 but was acquired from Cleverly, Cwmbran, in March 1992; it was sold in August 1993. Allocated to Pengam depot, it was on the Cardiff to Bargoed service when seen in May 1992.

Transferred from Bedwas depot to Porth in January 1996, Rhondda Buses 478 (YDW 400T) was still carrying Caerphilly Busways livery when photographed on the Cardiff to Tonypandy service in August 1996. YDW 400T, a Leyland National 10351A/1R, had been new as National Welsh NS1478 in July 1979, arriving with Rhondda Buses (via Tellings-Golden Miller) in May 1992. It passed to a dealer in February 1998 and was scrapped.

Rhondda Buses 861 (JHE 156W) was an MCW Metrobus DR104/6, with MCW H46/31F body, which had been new to South Yorkshire PTE in February 1981. It arrived at Rhondda Buses in August 1992 and departed for Merseyside in May 1994. Seen in Cardiff bus station in April 1994 it had arrived from Maerdy, a small town at the head of the Rhondda Fach valley.

Originally registered B176 FFS by Alexander Fife in December 1984 and carrying an Alexander double-deck coach body, Rhondda Buses 704 (A14 RBL) had a Volvo B10M-50 chassis and was acquired from Western Scottish in January 1995. It was sent for rebodying with this East Lancs DP53F body that November; it had just been re-registered A14 RBL when seen in Cardiff in January 1996.

An unusual addition to the Rhondda Buses fleet was 705 (A15 RBL), a Volvo B10M-56 with a Van Hool B51F body. It had been new to Hutchison, Overtown, registered B947 ASU in November 1984 and was acquired by Rhondda Buses from Henderson, Hamilton, in June 1995, gaining registration A15 RBL in January 1996. Photographed in August 1997, it was transferred to Red & White in December 1997.

New to South Wales Transport in June 1979, Leyland National 11351A/1R 808 (WWN 808T) was carrying the post-privatisation livery when seen at Pontardawe's Ammanford outstation in May 1987. It passed to Brewer in September 1993 and was sold in February 1995.

Two of the smaller vehicles in the South Wales Transport fleet were seen at Swansea's Quadrant bus station in July 1988. 72 (B172 BEP) was an Iveco 60-10 with a Robin Hood DP19F body, which served from February 1985 until July 1990. 71 (B171 BEP) was a Ford Transit with a Deansgate twelve-seat conversion which served from January 1985 until early 1992.

Many of South Wales Transport's minibus fleet gained roof-top advertising boards as seen on 241 (D241 LCY) at Swansea's Quadrant bus station. This was a Mercedes Benz L608D with Robin Hood B20F body new in October 1986 and sold in July 1998.

For many years South Wales Transport provided National Express services from west Wales; 164 (G164 LWN) was a Volvo B10M-60 new in April 1990 with a Plaxton Paramount 3500 Expressliner C46FT body. It was seen in Cardiff bus station, on service 625 to Gatwick Airport, in August 1990.

New to Eastern National in 1983 but acquired from Thamesway in July 1990, Brewer's 183 (HHJ 379Y) was an Alexander TE C53F-bodied Leyland Tiger TRCTL11/2R which was about to depart Cardiff for Swansea on the X1 in August 1993. HHJ 379Y passed to South Wales Transport as number 193, in April 1998, when the Brewer operation was merged with the parent company.

United Welsh Coaches operated as a separate company in the South Wales Transport group between December 1988 and September 1992 when it merged with Brewer. U74 (B993 CHG), a Mercedes Benz L608D with Coachcraft C21F body, had been new to Winder, Blackpool, in January 1985 registered B771 LPD, later 2428 WW. It became B993 CHG on sale to South Wales Transport; it had been transferred to United Welsh when photographed in June 1989.

United Welsh Coaches U176 (SWN 159) was a Leyland Tiger TRCTL11/3RZ with Plaxton Paramount 3500 II C49FT coachwork, which had been new to National Travel (East) in January 1985 registered B34 UNW. Acquired by United Welsh in January 1989, it received registration SWN 159, which had originally been carried by a 1959 Bristol Lodekka that February. It was seen at Gordano Services on the M5 motorway in July 1991.

United Welsh Coaches U139 (D400 GHT) shows the later livery carried; it was a Leyland Royal Tiger with Leyland's own C49FT bodywork which had been new as Badgerline 2400 in December 1986 and acquired by United Welsh in March 1990. Seen in Cardiff in May 1992, it passed to Brewer in August 1992. Re-registered YBK 132 in April 1993, it left the fleet in January 1996.

Clwyd Independent Operators

H78 CFV was a Mercedes Benz Vario 811D with Alexander AM B31F bodywork that had been new as Burnley & Pendle number 78 in April 1991. It was acquired by Davies of Bettws Gwerfil Goch, who used the fleet name G.H.A. Coaches, in November 1999 and was seen in Chester on service 17 from Handford in September 2000. It was time expired in March 2011.

New to Hanmer of Southsea, near Wrexham, in September 1991, Dennis Javelin 12SDA J730 KBC had a Plaxton Paramount 3200 C57F body. Seen in Cathays Park, Cardiff, in May 1993, it passed to Davies, Bettws Gwerfil Goch, in August 2000.

Hughes Transport of Rhyl acquired Alexander H47/32D-bodied Leyland Atlantean UKA 586H from Merseyside PTE in May 1982 – it had been ordered by Liverpool Corporation Transport Dept but was delivered after formation of the PTE. It was photographed in Rhyl in July 1982; the bus passed to Gold Star, St Asaph, by July 1985.

Jones & Towers of Flint purchased 1988 Van Hool Alizee C51FT-bodied DAF MB230LT615 F623 OHD from Welsh, Upton, West Yorkshire in 1991 and re-registered it BDM 81. Seen in Rutland Street, Leicester, on 1 May 1993 it was loading for the trip to the Spalding Flower Festival, where it and a couple of hundred other coaches would deposit its passengers to enjoy the annual flower parade.

Kerfoot-Davies of Dyserth used the fleet name Voel Coaches. VRP 60S was a Bristol VRT/SL3/6LXB with Alexander AL H45/27D bodywork that had been new to Northampton Corporation in October 1977, it passed to Kerfoot-Davies in July 1992 and was sold in October 2003. Although not traced after March 2004, its final road fund licence did not expire until December 2012! It was seen in Prestatyn bus station in September 2000.

P.&O. Lloyd of Bagillt 5182 PO was a Volvo B10M-61 with Van Hool Alizee C48FT coachwork. It had been new to Coupland, Fleetwood, registered VEC 55Y, in May 1983, passing to Hillman, Tredegar, in August 1988, where it was re-registered 3 MDH then UDW 427Y. It was acquired by Lloyd in June 1989 where it gained registration 5182 PO and the extra entrance door in the middle of the nearside. It was sold in January 1994.

RIL 3744 was a Volvo B10M-60 with Plaxton Paramount III C44FT body which, in September 2000, was operated by Owen of Denbigh who used the fleet name M&H. The coach had been new to Harry Shaw, Coventry, in April 1989 with registration F804 UDU, later carrying KOV 2 and F317 VVC. Owen ceased operation in May 2013.

Deva was the Roman name for Chester and Randall & Donnelly of Bretton used the fleet name Devaway. They had purchased PWT 274W, a 1981 Leyland PSU3F/4R with Willowbrook 003 C49F body from West Yorkshire PTE, where it had been numbered 2594, in July 1988. Seen in Chester in September 1992, its road tax was surrendered on 24 July 1996.

Randall & Donnelly's Leyland National 11351A/1R EUM 891T was in Chester bus station on the route to Mold in September 1992. Acquired from West Riding, where it had been number 190, in February 1991 its tax was surrendered in December 1997 and it was used for spares. Thus, both vehicles had left the fleet before the company was sold to Crosville Wales in March 1998.

Roberts of Cefn Mawr used the fleet name Vale of Llangollen Tours (hence the number of VLT registrations in the fleet) and was also contracted by Cosmos to carry its tour passengers. VLT 290 was a 1992 Volvo B10M-60 with a Jonckheere C51FT body, originally registered J459 HCA. Seen at Stonehenge in July 1997 it left the fleet in June 2000.

New to Volvo Bus at Irvine in January 1983, RSJ 814Y was a Volvo B10M-61 with a Plaxton Paramount 3500 I C51F body which was acquired by Roberts (Cloion Coaches) of Clawddnewydd from Jones, Pwllheli, in January 1992. Seen at the Albert Dock in Liverpool in September 1992, it was re-registered MIL 2180 in August 2001 and sold in January 2004.

Wright of Wrexham bought H256 YLG, a Leyland Lynx 2 with Leyland B49F bodywork new in November 1990; it was seen in Chester bus station in September 1992 operating the Wrexham to Chester service. The bus was sold to Cherry, Bootle, on Merseyside in February 1994.

Dyfed Independent Operators

New to Davies Bros of Pencader as fleet number 97 in May 1975, HBX 948N was a Bristol LH6L with ECW B45F bodywork. Sold in 1986, it was later exported to Malta. It was seen in Llandyssul on the Carmarthen service in June 1980.

New to Davies Bros of Pencader as number 142 in 1984, 2358 DD was a Leyland Tiger TRCTL11/3R with rare LAG Galaxy C49FT coachwork. It was re-registered A113 UDE on sale in 1990, later becoming 84-MH-505 with Fitzpatrick, Drumree, in the Republic of Ireland. It was seen at Charnock Richard services on the M6 in August 1988.

This magnificent machine is a Volvo B10M-53 6 × 2 with Plaxton Paramount 4000
CH53/9DT bodywork which was new as number 157 in the fleet of Davies Bros of
Pencader in August 1986. Originally registered D388 FBX, it became 6690 DD in
September 1987 but regained D388 FBX before sale in 1998. It was on a day trip to
Cardiff in March 1993.

Clive Edwards of Whitland used the fleet name Bysiau Cwm Taf (Taf Valley Buses)
and acquired Duple 340 C55F-bodied Leyland Tiger TRCTL11/3RZ E771 WSB
from East London, where it had been numbered TDL6, in October 1992. It was
re-registered NKH 819 in March 1993, just before it was caught parked up in Cardiff.

Jones of Llandeilo always turned out a well-presented coach. FTW 130T was a DAF MB200DKFL550 with Plaxton Supreme C49F body new to Harris, Grays, Essex, in April 1979. It was acquired by Jones in April 1985 and sold in October 1992. On 30 July 1992 it was in Cardiff bus station operating the National Express service to Birmingham.

A206 TAR was an AEC Reliance with Berkhof Esprite 340 C49F bodywork acquired by Jones of Llandeilo from East Kent in November 1989. It had been new to East Kent in 1973 registered HFN 54L and carrying a Duple body; the chassis was refurbished by Ensign in 1984 and the new Berkhof body fitted. April 1992 saw it in Cardiff operating a National Express service to Birmingham and carrying National Express livery.

Lewis of Rhydlewis bought 1987 Leyland Tiger TRCTL11/3RZ D65 MWO from Hills, Tredegar, in December 1991. It was fitted with a Plaxton Paramount 3500 III body and was re-registered 108 BDL in 1993; D156 JBX in 1998; and MIB 3230 in 2004. Sold for preservation in 2013, it had regained registration D156 JBX by August 2016.

Marchwood Motorways of Haverfordwest bought HPB 674N, a Bedford YRQ with Duple Dominant Bus B47F body, in April 1975 and gave it fleet number 42. It was seen in Haverfordwest in June 1980 and passed to Richards, Moylegrove, in September 1981. Marchwood closed its South Wales base in 1985, concentrating on its Hampshire operation.

The Postbus service from Llandovery to Myddfai commenced in July 1977 and Rootes eleven-seat Commer 2000LB OCY 702R was seen outside Llandovery post office on 31 August that year. It had Post Office fleet number 5750008 and carried lettering to indicate that it was sponsored by the Welsh Office. OCY 702R was replaced by similar Dodge Postbus KTH 824X (0750090) in August 1981.

Richards Brothers of Cardigan bought D983 OEJ, a DAF SB2300 with Duple 340 C53FT body, new in December 1986. It was seen in Cardiff in May 1993 and was sold in 2010.

Silcox of Pembroke Dock number 172 was E522 MDE, a Duple 425 integral coach with Dennis running units new in March 1988. Photographed in Hereford in September 1992, it was re-registered A2 WLS soon after but regained E522 MDE when sold in February 2003.

A16 WLS, Silcox of Pembroke Dock's number 116, was a Toyota Coaster HDB30R with Caetano Optimo II C21F body which had been new to Harry Shaw, Coventry, in March 1991 registered H75 HAW. It came to Silcox and was re-registered A16 WLS not long before I photographed it in Cardiff in September 1993. It became H59 JDE when sold in April 1996.

New to Thomas Bros of Llangadog in December 1970, OBX 125J was a Bedford VAS5 with Willowbrook B30F bodywork. Photographed in Llandovery, it stayed in the fleet until sold to Jones, Newchurch, in January 1981.

The Dennis Dorchester was quite rare, only sixty-seven being built, including Thomas Bros of Llangadog's VCY 401, which had a Plaxton Paramount 3200 I C53F body. It had been new to Johnson, Shaw, in Greater Manchester in August 1983 with registration A794 LCX, passing to Thomas Bros in September 1984 and gaining registration VCY 401 in 1987. It was in Cardiff Civic Centre in May 1993.

3201 MY was a Plaxton Paramount 3500 II C51FT-bodied Leyland Tiger TRCTL11/3R which had been new to Harry Shaw, Coventry, in June 1986 with registration C34 AVC. It was acquired by Williams & Thomas of Upper Tumble in 1991 as fleet number 25, gaining registration 3201 MY in December 1992. Williams & Thomas became Thomas & Pugh in May 1996 and the coach was seen in Cardiff in August 1997 operating a National Express service to Gatwick Airport.

Gwyn Williams of Lower Tumble's number 149 was Leyland Tiger TRCTL11/3LZ with Plaxton Bustler DP54F body registered E591 NBX. It had been new to the Ministry of Defence, in left-hand drive form, in September 1987 registered 87 KF 36. Acquired by Williams in March 1998 it was converted to right-hand drive and registered E591 NBX. Seen at Singleton Hospital, Swansea, in June 1998, it was time expired in September 2013.

Gwent Independent Operators

Clarke's Coaches of Tredegar had a twenty-year history. Commencing in March 1991 it took over the Globus contract from Hill's when they ceased later that year, but itself ceased operating in April 2011. Volvo B10M-62 N222 GLO was new in February 1996 with a Plaxton Premiere 350 C49FT body and was seen at Floors Castle, Scotland, in June 1997.

New to the Capitol fleet of Cleverly of Cwmbran in June 1980, FNY 331V was a Ford A0609 with Moseley Faro III C25F coachwork. Seen in its hometown in June 1988, it passed to Briggs, Swansea, by July 1990 and was later noted as a caravan in Morriston.

Another small vehicle from Cleverly of Cwmbran's Capitol fleet was 1989 Toyota Coaster HB31R G800 GHB, which carried the usual Caetano Optimo C21F body. It was seen in Cardiff in July 1992 and was withdrawn in March 1996 following an accident. It resurfaced in January 1997 with McNulty, Belmullet, in the Republic of Ireland re-registered 89-MO-3397.

Graham Davies of Tredegar used the fleet name Grahams and E806 HTF from the fleet was caught in Cardiff in March 1993. It was a Mercedes Benz Vario 811D with a Reeve Burgess C25F body that had been new to Ash, High Wycombe, in April 1988 and acquired by Davies in February 1991. It was re-registered PBZ 1403 in August 1996 and sold in February 2004. Grahams ceased operations early in 2016.

Fox of Blackwood used the fleet name Gwent Transport Services (G.T.S.) and purchased OKY 59R from Perry, Bromyard, in April 1990. It was a Leyland Leopard PSU3D/4R with Willowbrook 008 Spacecar C47F bodywork new to National Travel (North East) in 1977. Seen at Garden Festival Wales, Ebbw Vale, in May 1992, the coach was re-registered XWO 607 that July; it passed to Wacton, Bromyard, in January 1994 and was scrapped.

NIL 8654 was new to Bebb Travel, Llantwit Fardre, in October 1993 registered L53 CNY, making its way to the Gwent Omnibus Co. of Pontypool in November 1996 and being re-registered in October 1997. Seen at Barry Island in May 1998 carrying Phil Anslow Coaches lettering (Gwent OC being an associated company of Anslow), it reverted to L53 CNY that December and left the fleet in April 2000.

Also at Barry Island, in May 1998, was Gwent Omnibus Co.'s TJI 4123, a 1984 Duple Dominant Bus-bodied Leyland Tiger TRCTL11/2R which had been new to Trefaldwyn, Montgomery, as B472 ENT. Acquired from Bennett, Gloucester, in February 1998, it was re-registered TJI 4123 the following month. It regained B472 ENT on sale in January 2002 and was finally time expired in February 2017.

New to Hills of Tredegar in March 1989, Leyland Tiger TRCL10/3ARZM F597 BTG was fitted with a Plaxton Paramount 3500 C51FT body. It was seen on tour at Grasmere in the Lake District in August 1991 carrying Globus Gateway lettering and, following the closure of the Hills business, it passed to Anslow, Garndiffaith, in December 1991.

Lane of Tredegar ran as Gary's and in June 1991 bought D192 ESC, a 1987 MCW Metroliner DR130/33 with CH53/14DT bodywork. Originally an Eastern Scottish vehicle, it arrived via Safeguard, Guildford. Seen at the Garden Festival Wales site at Ebbw Vale in May 1992, it was re-registered A5 GJL that September and sold in 1994 being re-registered D436 OWO.

New to Lane of Tredegar in August 1998, Mercedes Benz Vario O814D S611 HGD had a Mellor C33F body. Seen at Gordano services on the M5 in July 2000, it was re-registered A15 DRW in March 2002 and S611 HGD in May 2007. It was out of service by July 2017.

Operated by Nutley of Caerwent, but carrying Jeff Nutley of Caldicot lettering, LTY 554X was a 1982 Bedford YNT with Plaxton Supreme V C53F coachwork acquired from Moor-Dale, Newcastle, in December 1987. Seen at the Wentwood Hotel near Caldicot in September 1991, the coach was sold to Evans, Tregaron, in September 1992.

Pedigree Travel of Abertillery was short-lived, only operating from around 1992 to early 1994. The first coach (of three) operated was Bova Futura FHD12-280 TSU 601, which had C49FT bodywork and was new to Silver Coach Lines in Edinburgh in March 1984, registered AJF 68A. In July 1993 it had returned home, being photographed at Holyroodhouse in Edinburgh.

Rees of Llanelly Hill near Abergavenny was in business by 1949 and purchased B292 RJF, a Bova Europa EL28/581 with C49FT bodywork, from County Travel, Leicester, in February 1990. It had been new to Housden, Loughborough, in 1985 registered B244 YKX, becoming 1661 PP in December 1988 and B292 RJF in November 1989. Seen in Cardiff in May 1992, it stayed in the Rees fleet until 2005.

Another short-lived Gwent operator was Roderick & Green of Brynmawr who were in business from 1988 to 1993 as Valley Coachways. B140 DAV, acquired in March 1989 from Abridge, Hadleigh, Essex, as their second vehicle was a DAF SB3000 with Jonckheere Jubilee P599 C53FT bodywork. It was on tour at Grasmere in August 1991.

Bernard Webley of Abertillery used the fleet name Bernies and operated three minibuses between December 1996 and December 2000. Mercedes Benz L508D NIL 3267 had a Devon Conversions C19F body and had been new to Hutchinson, Arborfield Cross, in 1982 with registration LMW 970X. It was at Barry Island in May 1998.

Glyn Williams of Crosskeys bought Dormobile B25F-bodied Mercedes Benz 709D L920 UGA in August 1993 and gave it fleet number 6. On 15 May 1994, when seen in Cardiff bus station, it was operating the tendered Sunday X17 service between Cardiff and Blackwood. The bus passed to Anslow, Pontypool, in June 1997 and Glyn Williams sold out to Red & White in February 2006.

Gwynedd Independent Operators

Acquired by Hughes Brothers of Llandudno in May 2000, Robin Hood B25F-bodied Mercedes Benz 709D F216 DCC came from Crosville Wales where it was numbered MMM216. In September 2000, it was covering the top section of the Great Orme Tramway while that was under renovation in preparation for its centenary in 2002.

New in August 1989 as a Carlyle demonstrator, G222 EOA, a Mercedes Benz 811D with Carlyle B31F body, was purchased by Jones of Bontnewydd in April 1992. Jones used the fleet name Express Motors, but G222 EOA was branded as the Porthmadog Clipa. Seen in a damp Pothmadog in September 2000, the bus was re-registered LUI 4744 a year later and sold in early 2003.

Seen in Porthmadog in September 2000, carrying Caelloi Cymru lettering, Jones of Pwllheli's N418 EJC was a Volvo B10M-62 with Plaxton Premiere 350 C49FT coachwork, which had been new in May 1996. It was sold in early 2001 and later operated in Ireland with registration 96-KK-3657.

Morris of Llanrug operated an up-market coach fleet under the Arvonia identity and EOS E180Z M2 ARV, which had an EOS C49FT body, was on tour at the Friendly Hotel, Norwich, in June 1995 when it was just two months old. The coach was sold in 2004 and re-registered C5 GBG by its new owner.

By the time R2 ARV was delivered in June 1998, Morris of Llanrug had become
Arvonia Coaches Ltd. It was a MAN 18.310 with Noge Catalan 3.50 C48FT
coachwork, which lasted in the fleet until September 2002. It was on tour in Great
Yarmouth when photographed in June 1999.

Parry of Blaenau Ffestiniog used the fleet name Regina Coaches and purchased A36
EFF, a Plaxton Paramount 3500 I-bodied DAF MB200DKFL600 new in August 1983;
it was seen at Hilton Park services on the M6 in May 1992. The Parry business,
including this coach, passed to Hughes of Llandudno in August 1997.

Roberts of Rhandir, near Abergele, acquired J166 MKM from Roberts, Llanddulais, in May 1996. It was a Crystals DP20F-bodied Leyland-DAF 400, which had been new as a Crystals demonstrator in early 1992. Seen in Porthmadog in September 2000, it passed to Johnson, Horwich, in July 2001.

Thomas of Upper Llandwrog, near Caernarfon, bought E911 UNW, a 1988 Volvo B10M-61 with Plaxton Paramount 3500 III C48FT body, from Wallace Arnold, Leeds, in February 1992. Seen on tour at the Angel Hotel in Cardiff in May 1993, it was sold to Isaac, Morriston, in March 1998. Thomas moved to Caernarfon in 1996, became Silver Star Coach Holidays Ltd in 2000, and ceased operations at the end of 2012.

Mid Glamorgan Independent Operators

Optare Starrider B33F-bodied Mercedes Benz 811D H85 PTG arrived in the Bebb
Travel of Llantwit Fardre fleet in May 1991. That December it was operating a
Shoppers' Park & Ride service when seen in The Hayes, Cardiff. The bus was sold
to a Greater Manchester operator in March 1994 and Bebb Travel was sold to
Veolia in 2006.

New to Bebb Travel of Llantwit Fardre in August 1991, J47 SNY was a Leyland Tiger
TRCL10/3ARZM with Plaxton 321 C53F body. In 1992 the coach was used as a
car park shuttle at the Garden Festival Wales site in Ebbw Vale. The Duple 320 body
became the Plaxton 321 when Plaxton took over production.

New to Bebb Travel in August 1994, M28 HNY was a Volvo B12T with Jonckheere Deauville 65 C47FT body. Seen in Cardiff bus station in April 1996 picking up for a holiday tour, the coach was sold that August. In later years, Bebb Travel would concentrate on the service bus and National Express operations.

R39 AWO was new to Bebb Travel in August 1997. A Setra S250 Special with C44FT coachwork, it was in Cardiff bus station on the second of the month loading for Bristol on National Express Rapide 301 service. The coach was sold in November 1999.

Len Hopkins was the fleet name used by Broadwest of Ogmore Vale and GFO 770X, a Bedford YNT with Duple Dominant III Express C53F body, was new to them in August 1981. It was in Cardiff in May 1992 for a choral event at the National Stadium. The Broadwest business closed in September 1998.

Another Ogmore Vale operator was Burrows who acquired ANA 458Y, a DAF MB200DKFL600 with Plaxton Paramount 3200 I C51F body, in July 1990. It had been new to Jacksons, Altrincham, in 1983. Burrows re-registered it TIB 6809 in 1993 and sold it in 1996. It was at Garden Festival Wales in Ebbw Vale in May 1992.

Edwards of Llantwit Fardre's YAP 104 was a DAF MB200DKVL600 with Jonckheere Jubilee P50 C53FT bodywork. It had been new to Roman City, Bath, in 1985 with registration B495 CBD, passing to Edwards in December 1986 and being re-registered in March 1991. It was seen at Jamaica Inn, Bolventor, in October 1997.

MWW 751K was operated by Evans of New Tredegar between November 1989 and August 1995. New to West Yorkshire Road Car Co. as number 1358 in February 1972, it was a Bristol RELL6G with ECW B53F bodywork. It was operating a Merthyr Tydfil local service when seen in May 1990.

Cyril Evans of Senghenydd was a long-established company which ceased operations in January 1999. RMA 314P, a 1976 Leyland Leopard PSU3C/4R with Plaxton Supreme III Express C49F body, was acquired from Crosville, where it was numbered ELL314 in February 1988. Despite the lettering on the front, it appeared to be operating the Abertridwr service (note the Mill Road label in the windscreen) when seen in Caerphilly bus station in March 1989.

G&A Travel of Caerphilly bought CWO 116V, a 1979 Bedford YMT with Plaxton Supreme IV C53F body, from Evans, Senghenydd, in April 1990. It was laying over in Westgate Street, Cardiff, in May 1992 and left the fleet that September.

Gareth Handy of Merthyr Tydfil used the fleet name Sixty-Sixty Coaches and many of his vehicles received 6060 registrations. FBZ 6060 was a 1978 Ford R1114 with a Plaxton Supreme III C53F body that had been new to Allenways, Birmingham, with registration VRY 730S. It was waiting for a wedding party when photographed in its hometown in May 1993.

Howarth of Merthyr Tydfil used the fleet name Silverline and bought E163 OMD new in May 1988. It was a Leyland Swift LBM6T/2RS with Wadham Stringer Vanguard DP37F bodywork and was sold to Pioneer, St Helier, Jersey, in November 1995. Silverline was acquired by Handy in 1997, some vehicles then received 60-60 Silverline branding.

Jones of Pontypridd used the fleet name Shamrock to cover various companies in the group. CVE Omni B23F F976 WEF was new to CVE, Shildon, as a demonstrator in March 1989 and had recently been acquired by Jones when operating a Shoppers' Park & Ride service in Cardiff in late 1993.

An unusual vehicle in the Jones (Shamrock), Pontypridd, fleet was L957 JGS, an Iveco TurboCity-U with a Wadham Stringer B47F body. It had been a demonstrator and was acquired in September 1994 when just four months old. Seen in Cardiff bus station in July 1995 on the Aberdare service, it was sold in February 2006.

Kerslake of Caerphilly used the fleet name Castell Coaches and acquired PTV 593X from Barton, Chilwell, in 1987. It was a Bedford YNT with Plaxton Supreme IV Express C53F body which had been new in 1981. Photographed under a threatening sky in Caerphilly, in May 1988, the coach departed for pastures new in January 1992.

In August 1991, Kerslake of Caerphilly was using Mercedes Benz Vario 811D E76 LRN, which had a Reeve Burgess Beaver C33F body, on the Cardiff Bay Tour. This was a free service, operated on behalf of the Cardiff Bay Development Corporation to allow the public to view the regeneration work being carried out. E76 LRN was seen in Cardiff docklands.

Mainwaring of Tonyrefail used the Mainline fleet name and had this attractive light green livery. Volvo B10M-60 F42 LTO had a Plaxton Paramount 3200 C57F body. It had been new to Skill, Nottingham, in 1989. Purchased by Mainwaring in March 1991, it stayed in the fleet until January 2013. It was seen at Gordano services on the M5 motorway in August 1994.

Morgan of Trelewis used the fleet names Acorn Mini Travel and Acorn Travel. An early vehicle in this fleet was this Iveco TurboDaily 45-10 with a B16FL body, which was seen at Barry Island in May 1998. Registration 592 DCJ went on to grace a number of Morgan's coaches, but the original identity of this one remains unknown.

Morris Travel of Pencoed acquired NTD 116K with the Coity Motors business of John, Coity, in May 1985. New to Lancaster City Transport in 1972, it was a Leyland PSU3B/2R with a Pennine B51F body. Although this is a June 1987 view in Bridgend bus station, the bus still carries the Coity name. It left the fleet for a Lancashire operator in late 1990.

This neat Dennis Javelin 8.5SDA with Plaxton Paramount 3200 C35F body was new to Parfitt of Rhymney Bridge in April 1992 and sold in May 1995, just after the company had been taken over by Rhondda Buses. I caught up with it at Gordano services on the M5 in August 1994.

Entering service with WG Thomas of Clydach Vale in August 1988, F334 YTG was a DAF SBR3000DKSB570 with a Berkhof Excellence 2000HD CH59/17CT body. It was on a private hire when seen at Frankley services on the M5 in September 1988 and was sold in March 1994.

Waddon of Bedwas (formerly at Caerphilly) acquired 551 FVW from Eglington, Sittingbourne, in January 1989. It was a Ford R1114 with Plaxton Supreme C53F body which had been new to Parks, Hamilton, with registration NGB 23P in March 1976. It was waiting for its passengers in Cardiff bus station in September 1990.

John Williams of Porthcawl had acquired the Porthcawl Omnibus Company by June 1989 and Volvo B10M-61 LNV 795, which had a Jonckheere Bermuda C49FT body, was seen in that livery in Cardiff in February 1992. LNV 795 had been new to Club Cantabrica, St Albans, in May 1980 with registration GPA 628V. It joined the Williams fleet in July 1989.

John Williams' Porthcawl Omnibus Co. fleet acquired B813 JPN, a 1985 Leyland Tiger TRCTL11/3RH with Duple Caribbean C50F body from Oare, Brynford, Clwyd, in May 1993. It had been new as Southdown 1013 in 1985. Williams sold the coach in April 1995 and its road tax was finally surrendered in May 2011. B813 JPN was in Cardiff bus station in June 1993 on the company's X14 Cardiff to Porthcawl via Bridgend service.

Powys Independent Operators

Brown of Builth Wells operated Bedford YRT HBW 873N from 1988 to 1993; it had a Plaxton Panorama Elite C53F body. New to Heyfordian, Upper Heyford, in November 1974, it spent 1981 to 1987 with the Army under registration 59 BT 55. It was seen in Hereford bus station in September 1992.

New to Brown of Builth Wells in February 1994, L710 LFO was a Toyota Coaster HZB50R with Caetano Optimo III C21F body. It was seen at Barry Island in June 1999 and left the fleet in March 2000.

Cross Gates Coaches was formed in January 1989 from the erstwhile Knill of Cross Gates operation. KGA 316N was a 1975 Bristol LHS6L with Plaxton Supreme C33F coachwork acquired from Jones, Macclesfield, in April 1989 and sold in October 1993. It was caught in Hereford bus station in September 1992.

Cross Gates Coaches 7074 DK had been new to Hills, Tredegar, in March 1982 with registration NDW 142X. It was a Leyland Tiger TRCTL11/2R with a Plaxton Supreme VI Express C53F body, acquired and re-registered by Cross Gates in August 1991. It was seen in Cardiff Civic Centre in May 1993.

Bob Davies of Talgarth used the fleet name Talgarth Travel. 914 JOW was a Leyland Leopard PSU5D/4R with a Plaxton Supreme C48FT body, which had been new to Rickards, Brentford, with registration XGS 772X in August 1981. Seen in Cardiff in May 1993, this coach was sold in March 1995 and, presumably, scrapped. Davies ceased operations in 2002.

Jones of Llanidloes used the fleet name Celtic Travel and purchased Volvo B10M-61 A606 UGD from Park, Hamilton, in 1988. It had a Van Hool Alizee C49FT body and had been new in February 1984. Photographed in Cardiff in May 1992, the coach was withdrawn by August 2014.

Still carrying Joseph Jones, Ystradgynlais, livery when photographed in March 1993, YTH 930T had passed to Long of Abercraf when Joseph Jones ceased operations in May 1990. It was a Leyland Leopard PSU3E/4R with Plaxton Supreme IV Express C53F body which had been new to Thomas, Llangadog, in August 1979. Re-registered OIL 4470 in March 1998, it had become a mobile caravan by December 2003.

Long of Abercraf acquired this Iveco (Fiat) 60-10 with Caetano Baja C18F body from Hammond, Luton, in March 1992. It had been new to Hodge, Sandhurst, Berkshire, in December 1981 with registration TNR 794X. The operator became Long & Evans in November 1992 and sold out to Veolia in October 2006, the vehicles being transferred to the Pullman licence.

Williams had been based in Cwmdu when Reeve Burgess C19F-bodied Mercedes Benz 608D D449 BFO entered service in April 1987 but moved to Brecon in 1991. Photographed at Hilton Park services on the M6 motorway in July 1993, D449 BFO was re-registered IIL 8520 in April 1996 and sold in September 1998.

Another coach acquired by Williams when based at Cwmdu was this 1981 Leyland Leopard PSU5D/5R with Duple Dominant III C53F body, which had been new to Titterington, Blencow, Cumbria, registered OWF 692X. Arriving from Bevan, Lydney, in October 1984, it received registration 6654 HA in 1985. It was photographed in Westgate Street, Cardiff, in January 1990.

South Glamorgan Independent Operators

Cardiff Bluebird 67 (ONN 574P) was acquired from Trent, where it had been numbered 574, in November 1994. A Leyland Atlantean AN68/1R, it carried a full-height ECW H43/31F body and had been new in July 1976. ONN 574P passed to Cardiff Bus in September 1996, but like all the former Cardiff Bluebird vehicles was not operated. Photographed in Firs Avenue, Pentrebane, on 26 June 1995.

Cardiff Bluebird only bought two new vehicles. They were 1995 Dennis Dart 9.5SDLs 1/2 (M100/200 CBB), which had Plaxton Pointer B40F bodywork, and 2 (M200 CBB) was seen in Wood Street in March 1995. These vehicles did not pass to Cardiff Bus, but went to Maidstone & District where they were numbered 3474/5.

City Centre of Cardiff acquired Duple 340 C50FT-bodied Leyland Tiger TRCTL10 E450
MMM from Tellings-Golden Miller, Cardiff, in June 1991. It had been new to CTC,
Caerphilly, in 1988. Photographed in December 1991, it was sold in July 1993 to Nesbit,
Somerby, Leicestershire, and was time-expired in April 2010.

FKM 91V entered the R. Evans of Cardiff fleet in January 1987, being bought from Devon
operator Nightingale at Budleigh Salterton. It was a 1979 Ford R1114 with Caetano Alpha
C46FT coachwork. Photographed in Cardiff bus station in August 1989, it lasted in the
fleet until early 1995.

Forster of Cardiff used the fleet name Croeso Tours and acquired A792 RSN from
Strathmartine, Dundee, in 1989. It was an Iveco (Fiat) 60F10 with a Caetano Baja
C18F body that had been new in August 1983. Caught at Gordano services on the
M5 motorway in June 1991, this little coach passed to Walton, Grangetown, Cardiff,
in April 2002.

Golden Coaches started up at Cwmaman in 1988 moving to Llandow in 1990. E700
HLB was a Mercedes Benz 609D with Reeve Burgess C23F body new in March 1988.
Seen in Cardiff bus station operating the Llantwit Major service in August 1990, it
was sold in 1994.

The only double-decker operated by Golden Coaches of Llandow was Bristol VRT/ SL3/6LXB UGR 693R, which had been new to United Automobile in 1976 but was acquired from Northumbria in September 1993. Seen on the Cardiff to Llantwit Major service in April 1994, it was withdrawn that June but remained in the fleet until the company ceased operations in February 1995.

Grisedale & Hart of Roath, Cardiff, used the fleet name Venture Travel. Daimler CRG6LXB YNA 299M had a Northern Counties H43/32F body and had been new to SELNEC PTE in November 1973, being acquired (by predecessor company Grisedale & Griffiths) from Cleverly, Cwmbran, in November 1989. It was seen in Pentrebane, Cardiff, in March 1994 waiting to operate a school service.

Tellings-Golden Miller of Cardiff operated C570 TUT, a Dormobile B16F-bodied Ford Transit between July 1991 and July 1992. I caught up with it in Cardiff bus station just before it was sold. New to Midland Fox in 1986, it was transferred from Tellings-Golden Miller at Byfleet. The Cardiff operation became Cardiff Bluebird in 1995.

Seen in Cardiff bus station on its first day in service, 1 May 1992, Tellings-Golden Miller's J247 MFP was a Volvo B10M-60 with Plaxton Paramount 3500 C46FT bodywork in National Express Rapide livery. It had only a short stay in the Cardiff fleet, being transferred to the Byfleet operation in September 1992.

Staying in the Thomas Motors of Barry fleet for less than a month, A60 OJX was a Bedford YNT with Wright Contour C53F coachwork new to Traject, Huddersfield, in February 1984. Seen in Cardiff Civic Centre in July 1986 it was sold later the same month and later operated for Helms of Eastham on Merseyside.

Thomas Motors of Barry acquired Leyland National 1151/2R/0403 JHU 850L from Bristol Omnibus Co. in March 1990. By the time I photographed it in Mill Lane, Cardiff, in August 1993 working the 304 service back to its hometown, it had been converted from B44D to B48F. Although withdrawn in April 1995, it passed to the Shamrock organisation in January 1996 as a source of spare parts.

Basil Walton of Grangetown, Cardiff, was in business by 1965 and in July 1987 bought ANB 757Y from Greater Manchester Police. It was a Duple Dominant C53F-bodied Ford R1114, which had been new in January 1983. ANB 757Y stayed in the fleet until late 1998. The company is still in business, being run by Russell Walton.

Ernest Wheadon of Cardiff started operations in 1982 and in March 1990 bought D764 TDV, a shortened Bedford YMP with Plaxton Paramount III C35F body, which had been new to Seward, Dalwood, Devon, in April 1987. Seen in Hayes Bridge Road, Cardiff, in May 1992, it operated in Cardiff Bay Tours livery and was sold in April 1995.

West Glamorgan Independent Operators

The Leyland Tiger TRCL10/3RZA chassis of D Coaches of Morriston's F682 SRN was new to Leyland Motors Research Dept in March 1987, being bodied with this Plaxton Paramount 3500 III C51FT body in March 1988 and registered in August 1988 as a Leyland demonstrator. Sold to D Coaches in December 1990 it was caught on tour at Lynmouth in June 1991. It left the fleet in February 1994.

Still in 'as acquired' livery when seen on tour in Llandudno in September 2000, D Coaches of Morriston had acquired J500 CCH, a 1992 Volvo B10M-60 with Berkhof Excellence 2000 C50FT body, from Cantabrica, St Albans, in May 1998. D Coaches and the associated Diamond Holidays closed in January 2011. Parts of the business were acquired by Edwards of Llantwit Fardre.

Fussell & Gower of Swansea used the fleet name Millbrook Mini Coaches and in December 1999 acquired KCX 7W, a shortened Bedford YMQ with Duple Dominant IV C35F body that had been new in 1981. It was seen at Leckwith Stadium, Cardiff, in June 2000 and was sold by December 2003.

Brian Isaac of Morriston acquired former East Kent Iveco (Fiat) Daily 49-10 J114 LKO in August 1997. It had a Carlyle B23F body and had been new in November 1991. It was at Swansea's bus station in August 1990 when operating a service to the marina.

New to Jenkins of Skewen in January 1982, Plaxton Supreme V C53F-bodied Volvo
B10M-61 LWN 126X was on tour in Brixham when photographed in June 1989.
Jenkins had been acquired by Smiths Shearings of Wigan in December 1988 and this
coach was numbered 376 in their fleet. Sold in December 1989, it was finally time
expired in September 2006.

Carrying Jenkins of Skewen fleet names, the livery and fleet number (348) indicate
that this is a Smiths Shearings vehicle. C348 DND, a Volvo B10M-61 with Plaxton
Paramount 3200 II C53F body, new to Smith, Wigan, in March 1986, operated from
Skewen from April 1989 and was seen about to pick up tour passengers from Cardiff
bus station in July 1989.

I. Jones of Pontardawe used the fleet name Glantawe Coaches and purchased DAF MB200DKTL600 RTH 102Y new in March 1983. It was fitted with a Caetano Alpha GT C49FT body and received registration GJM 881 in March 1984. It was picking up in Cardiff bus station in May 1994 and passed to D Coaches, Morriston, with the Glantawe business in January 1996.

I. Jones of Pontardawe's DDZ 1639 had started life with Roman City, Bath, in August 1984 registered B500 CBD. It was a DAF SBR2300DHS585 with Jonckheere Jubilee P99 CH57/14CT body. Acquired by Jones in April 1989, it was re-registered DDZ 1639 in May 1991. Seen travelling through Wood Street, Cardiff, in May 1993, it also passed to D Coaches in January 1996.

NWD 558P was a Bedford YMT with Duple Dominant C53F body, which had been new to National Travel (Midlands) in June 1976. It arrived with Margam Cabs in March 1993, the Blue Rambler fleet name coming from its previous owner, Ellis & Lewis, Cliftonville, Kent. Seen at Garden Festival Wales, Ebbw Vale, in May 1992, it was burnt out in August 1996.

Merlyns of Skewen operated IUI 2173 from August 1997. New to Londoners Tacho, SE5, in 1984 it was a Volvo B10M-61 with Plaxton Paramount 3500 C49FT body. Originally registered A368 YME, it became IUI 2173 in May 1997 via various other registrations. Photographed at Cardiff's Leckwith Athletics Stadium in June 2000 it was sold in November 2003. Merlyns was acquired by Pullman, Crofty, in 2004.

Morriston Coaches of Morriston near Swansea bought DLX 32Y, a 1983 Scania K112CRS with Jonckheere Jubilee P50 C51FT body, from Horseshoe, London, N15, in May 1988 and re-registered it AEF 367A that August. It was seen at Chievely services on the M4 in July 1990. Morriston Coaches ceased operations in October 1991 and the coach passed to the dealer Moseley.

Pullman of Crofty acquired 572 RKJ in January 1993. It was an MCW Metroliner CR126/2 with C51F bodywork that had been new to East Kent with registration FKK 846Y in 1983. Seen at Gordano services on the M5 in July 1993, it left the fleet in February 1995. The Pullman business was acquired by Veolia in 2006.

E613 AEY of Pullman of Crofty was a Duple 425 C51FT integral coach with Dennis running units. New to Crosville Wales with fleet number CDC3 in June 1988, it was acquired from Amberline on Merseyside in July 1993. It was at Leigh Delamere services on the M4 in June 1995 and was sold to dealer Kirkby that December. It was time expired in August 2009.

Darren Ridgway of Port Talbot acquired B906 DHB, a Leyland Tiger TRCTL11/3R with Duple Caribbean 2 C51FT coachwork, from Brewer in September 1996 and re-registered it 111 BWO in May 1997. The coach had been new to Cardiff in June 1985 as fleet number 6 and passed to Brewer in October 1995 with Cardiff Buses' excursion and private hire business. Seen at Barry Island in June 1999, it was sold in September 2003.

Tonna Luxury Coaches used the fleet name Ken Hopkins and purchased Volvo B58-56 WSW 150V from Smith, Rayne, Essex, in May 1992, re-registering it XXI 7360 in September 1992. Fitted with a Duple Dominant II C53F body it had been new to Little, Annan, in Dumfries & Galloway in March 1980. Seen in Cathays Park, Cardiff, in May 1993, it was time expired in October 2000.

Warren of Neath used the fleet name Bluebird Coaches, but many of their coaches ran in Majestic Holiday Tours colours. K841 HUM was a 1993 Volvo B10M-60 with Jonckheere Deauville 45 C50F bodywork, which was acquired from Wallace Arnold Coaches in May 1997. In July 2000 it was on tour to the Isle of Wight and was seen outside the Carlton Hotel in Sandown.

Showing Warren of Neath's Bluebird Coaches fleet name, Volvo B10M-60 KUI 2759 had a Plaxton Paramount 3500 C53F body and was new to Park, Hamilton, in March 1989 with registration F981 HGE. The coach arrived with Warren in March 2000 and was immediately re-registered KUI 2769. Seen in Llandudno in September 2000, it was sold to Law, Shotts, in March 2004.

Wilkins of Cymmer in the Afan Valley acquired all-Leyland Royal Tiger C53F E51 TYG from West Riding in March 1989, when it was only twelve months old, and operated it in the West Riding livery. Seen in Cardiff in July 1989, it was re-registered 551 FVW in February 1997 and stayed in the fleet until mid-2007.

Non-PSV Operators

Two Bedford VAS5s of Mid Glamorgan County Council Social Services Dept photographed in Caerphilly in July 1991. C750 HHB of 1986 had a locally built Thomas Hosking body and D869 FTR of 1987 had a Wadham Stringer Vanguard body. Both are thought to have been sold prior to the 1996 Local Government Reorganisation.

Seen near the Claerwen Dam in the Elan Valley in May 1988, Plaxton Embassy-bodied Bedford SB5 324 FOF was a snack bar owned by a Mr Davies. New to Myatt, Birmingham, in 1962, it served snacks from July 1982 until 1990 when it became a caravan with hippies.

New to Powys County Council Education Dept in March 1977, Bedford VAS5 MEJ 412R carries one of four known bus bodies constructed by Jones of Llanidloes (the other three being similar to this one). Seen at Brecon in June 1978, its road tax was surrendered in August 1986.

Burges House in Roath, Cardiff, was one of a national chain of homes catering for the elderly. It operated H406 KPY, a long CVE Omni, from September 1990 until August 2000. It was seen near the home in July 1993.

Seen outside the National Museum of Wales in Cathays Park, Cardiff, in August 1995 was South Glamorgan County Council Social Services Department's M676 SDB. This was a Mercedes Benz 609D with Cunliffe B8FL body which had been new in June 1995. The 1996 Local Government Reorganisation saw the bus passing to the Vale of Glamorgan Borough Council. It was exported in March 2011.

The St John Ambulance Brigade in Wales acquired 1970 Bristol LH6L POD 820H from Western National, where it had been numbered 761, in April 1984 and converted its ECW B43F body into a Mobile First Aid post. Seen attending a fun run in Bute Park, Cardiff, in July 1989, it appears to have been sold around April 1996.

New in April 1999 as a demonstrator, Cardiff International Airport's T343 FWR was an Optare Solo M850 with B26F body acquired from the manufacturer by June 2001. At this time, the airport was owned by private company TBI but was later bought by the Welsh Assembly Government. The bus passed to Shamrock, Pontypridd, in 2002 along with the car park shuttle service.

New to SELNEC PTE in November 1972, YDB 454L was a Seddon Pennine IV.236 with Seddon DP25F bodywork, originally numbered EX57 but later becoming 1701. UBM Scaffolding of Swansea acquired the bus from Greater Manchester PTE in 1978 and numbered it 9004. It was seen in Swansea in July 1980 and was sold by October 1983.